ENDANGERED!

RHINOCEROSES

Amanda Harman

Series Consultant: James G. Doherty
General Curator, The Bronx Zoo, New York

MARSHALL CAVENDISH
NEW YORK

Benchmark Books
Marshall Cavendish Corporation
99 White Plains Road
Tarrytown, New York 10591-9001

Library of Congress Cataloging-in-Publication Data

Harman, Amanda, 1968-
    Rhinoceroses / by Amanda Harman.
        p.   cm. — (Endangered!)
    Includes index.
    Summary: Describes the physical characteristics, habitat, and
behavior of white, black, Sumatran, Javan, and Indian rhinoceroses—
the five species of rhinos left in the world.
    ISBN 0-7614-0290-X (lib. bdg.)
    1. Rhinoceroses—Juvenile literature.   2. Endangered species—
Juvenile literature.   N. Rhinoceroses.   2. Endangered species.]
I. Title.   II. Series.
QL737.U63H37 1997
599.72'8—dc20   96-10863
                                                          CIP
                                                           AC

Printed and bound in the United States

PICTURE CREDITS
*The publishers would like to thank the Frank Lane Picture Agency (FLPA) for
supplying all the photographs used in this book except for the following: 4, 6,
7, 10, 14, 19, 20 Bruce Coleman Ltd; 12, 13, 28 Natural History Photographic
Agency; 25 Silvestris (via FLPA).*

Series created by Brown Packaging

Front cover: Black rhino.
Title page: Indian rhino.
Back cover: White rhinos.

Contents

Introduction

With their barrel-shaped bodies, short, thick legs, and huge, boxlike heads, rhinoceroses (or rhinos) are among the largest and heaviest land animals alive today. Their pointed horns and tough, thick, wrinkled hide make them look a little like dinosaurs, the great **reptiles** that ruled the Earth millions of years ago. But they are not reptiles. Rhinos are **mammals**, like their closest relatives, the elephants and the hippopotamus, and like human beings.

Millions of years ago, there were many different kinds of rhinos living on Earth. Some of these ancient rhinos were huge. One of them, known as baluchitherium (buh-loo-chi-THEER-i-uhm), was the largest land mammal ever. At

A black rhino feeds in the grasslands of Africa. The birds on its back are oxpeckers. They eat the insects living on the rhino's skin and those stirred up as it feeds.

more than 40,000 pounds (18,000 kg), it weighed as much as three fully grown elephants! Another ancient rhino was the woolly rhinoceros, which had a long, shaggy coat. This rhino lived in Asia and Europe until about 15,000 years ago, when it became **extinct**.

Today there are only five **species** of rhinos in the world. The white and black rhinos from Africa and the Sumatran, Javan, and Indian rhinos from Asia. Sadly, these rhinos are almost extinct, too. Their thick skin and fearsome horns cannot protect them from people and their guns. In this book we will look at all five species of rhinos – at how they live and at what **conservationists** are doing to stop these animals from disappearing forever in the wild. We will start with the African rhinos.

An Indian rhino stands in the elephant grass where it makes its home. With its "armor-plated" hide and the folds around its neck, this species is the most dinosaur-like of the rhinos.

AFRICA

Equator

Atlantic
Ocean

Indian
Ocean

Areas where the black rhino can be found

A charging black rhino is a terrifying sight. These huge, powerful animals have few enemies besides people.

African Rhinos

There are two species of African rhinos – the white and the black. The white is the bigger of the two, and male whites are the largest rhinos in the world today. They may weigh more than 5000 pounds (2300 kg) and measure up to 13 feet (4 m) long. Females are smaller and usually weigh about 3740 pounds (1700 kg) and measure about 11½ feet (3.6 m) in length.

It is easy to tell the white rhino from other rhinos by its unusually wide, square-shaped mouth and the large hump on the back of its neck. This contains the muscles to support its huge head. Despite its name, the white rhino is not white at all, but dark gray in color. Its two horns sit one behind the other on the front of its head. The smaller of the two sits just above its eyes, while the second horn grows at the end of the rhino's nose. Unlike those of antelope and sheep, rhino horns are made not of bone but of keratin (KER-a-tin). This is similar to the material from which our hair and fingernails are made.

A white rhino drinks at a waterhole. The white rhino's front horn is usually about 24 inches (61 cm) in length, though it may grow as long as 59 inches (1.5 m).

Areas where the
white rhino can
be found

*If the grass is
too short, the
white rhino
will often use
its front horn
to dig up the
grass roots
and eat them
instead.*

Like other large hoofed mammals, such as elephants and horses, rhinos are **herbivores**. This means that they do not eat any meat, but feed completely on plants. Because rhinos are so huge, they have to eat a large amount of plant matter just to stay alive and they usually feed for up to 15 hours a day. The white rhino is a **grazer**, and its wide, square-shaped mouth is specially **adapted** to allow it to eat short grasses.

Although they can survive for four to five days without water during the dry season, white rhinos prefer to drink every two or three days and will often walk up to 6 miles (9.6 km) to find a new waterhole. Rhinos also like to wallow, or roll around, in waterholes and small rivers. This, along with dust-bathing, helps them to stay cool, especially during the afternoon when the sun is at its hottest.

Female whites are unusual for rhinos in that they will sometimes live in groups of three to ten. On the other hand, males (called bulls) are solitary and live in a **territory** that they defend against other males. If a rival bull enters another's territory, the owner will approach the intruder.

White rhinos wallow at a mud pool. Besides keeping them cool, wallowing gives rhinos a thick coating of mud. This protects them from biting insects.

First, the two rhinos stand face to face, slowly raising their heads and touching horns. Then they back away from each other, with their heads bowed, and begin wiping their front horn on the ground, all the while pawing with their feet and snorting loudly. At this point, the intruder will usually give a high-pitched growl and retreat. If it does not, there may be a fight.

White rhinos live mainly on flat, grassy plains with lots of bushes and patches of trees. They can be found in

A young male white playfully tries out his strength on an older rhino. One day he may have to challenge a male intruder in his territory.

southern Africa, from Zambia down to South Africa, and in central Africa in Zaire's Garamba National Park. Rhinos from these two areas differ enough from one another for scientists to see them as two **subspecies** – the southern white rhino and the northern white rhino. There are now less than 6000 southern white rhinos. The northern white rhino is in even more serious danger. Today there are thought to be just 30 left.

Like the white rhino, the black rhino has a rather misleading name, since its skin is usually a slate-gray color. The black is a medium-sized rhino. Males and females do not differ much in size. Both measure about 10 feet (3 m) in length and weigh up to 2860

The black rhino is sometimes called the hook-lipped rhino because it has a long, movable upper lip. This helps it to grasp the leaves, shoots, and twigs that it feeds on.

pounds (1300 kg). Like the white rhino, the black has two horns: the front horn may be almost 4 feet (1.2 m) long, while the other one may measure up to 20 inches (50 cm). Unlike white rhinos, black rhinos feed by **browsing** on a wide variety of plants, shrubs, bushes, and trees.

The black rhino is regarded as the most aggressive of all the rhinos. If an animal, a person, or a vehicle gets too close, a black rhino will charge. It runs at the intruder to frighten it off, and if it goes away, the rhino will stop. If the intruder stays, though, the rhino will attack. Black rhinos are heavy and strong, and their horns can do serious damage even to a vehicle.

Black rhinos are fearless and will even charge big cats. This lion knows it must move away or the rhino will attack.

Some people say they have seen black rhinos charge for no reason at all. However, in these cases, it is likely that the rhino was startled. Like all rhinos, blacks can hear well and have an excellent sense of smell. But they are very shortsighted – if you stood 100 feet (30 m) from a black rhino and did not move, the rhino probably would not see you. This means that sometimes it is possible to get too close to a black rhino without its noticing. Scientists believe that when the rhino eventually realizes there is something nearby, it becomes frightened and charges.

Black rhinos spend most of their time alone, and males and females get together only to **mate**. Like other rhinos, they can breed at any time of year. The female goes in search of a male partner, signaling to him by spraying urine on the bushes and grass. He responds with a display that

A black rhino charges through its woodland home. Despite its size, a black rhino can reach speeds of up to 30 miles per hour (48 km/h).

may last for several hours. First, he rubs his front horn against the ground, sweeping his head from side to side. Then he charges backward and forward into the bushes, spraying urine as he does so. The female is very aggressive toward him at first, but eventually she accepts him.

About 15 months after mating, the female finds a sheltered spot to give birth to her offspring, usually a single calf. Baby rhinos are fairly well developed when they are born. Black rhinos, for example, weigh about 90 pounds (41 kg) at birth. The calf feeds on its mother's milk at first. Although it will begin to eat other food, such as grass, at about one week old, it will continue to drink milk for at

A pair of black rhinos get to know each other before mating. Sometimes males and females have "swordfights" with their horns at this time.

least 18 months. As the young rhino grows up, its mother teaches it everything it needs to know about where to find food and water, and where the best wallowing places are.

Black rhinos live in southern, central, and eastern Africa and can be found in a number of different **habitats**, from **rainforest** to wooded grassland. They can even survive in the Kalahari Desert. However, the number of black rhinos has fallen sharply over the past 30 years. In 1970, there were about 65,000 black rhinos throughout southern and eastern Africa. Now there are probably less than 2500 scattered over their **range**. This number is still dropping.

A young black rhino chews a mouthful of grass as it trots behind its mother. When it is about four years old, its mother will chase it away to start a life of its own.

Asian Rhinos

Three species of rhinos live in Asia – the Indian, the Javan, and the Sumatran. The Sumatran is the smallest of the three and the smallest rhino in the world. Weighing about 1760 pounds (800 kg), a Sumatran rhino usually measures about 10 feet (3 m) long and 4 feet 4 inches (1.3 m) high at the shoulders. Males and females are about the same size.

As well as being the smallest species, the Sumatran rhino differs from other rhinos in having a thick covering of hair all over its body. This makes many scientists think that it is the closest living relative of the extinct woolly rhinoceros.

The Sumatran rhino is a shy animal and rarely seen. It looks clumsy but can easily climb the steep tracks in the mountain forests in which it lives.

Like the African white rhino, the Sumatran rhino has two horns. Because it is the only rhino in Asia that does, it is often known as the Asian two-horned rhinoceros. In the female, both horns are fairly small, but in the male, the front horn, the larger of the two, may grow up to 15 inches (38 cm) long.

Sumatran rhinos were once widespread throughout Southeast Asia, but now there are only 450 to 800 left. They live in thick, **tropical** rainforests on the sides of

A male Sumatran rhino (front) and a female relax together. Sumatran rhinos have fairly small horns, which are not much use as weapons in fights.

mountains. They are often found in upland forests, as high as 6500 feet (2000 m).

The Javan rhino is larger than the Sumatran, measuring about 11½ feet (3.6 m) long and weighing about 3000 pounds (1400 kg). Males and females are generally about the same size. The Javan has only one small horn – usually less than 10 inches (25 cm) long – halfway along its snout, and is sometimes known as the lesser one-horned rhinoceros. Often, females have hardly any horn at all.

The Javan rhino is a distinctive-looking animal. It has the same heavy-set, barrel-shaped body of other rhinos, but its gray skin hangs in folds over its shoulders, back, and

Like the Javan rhino, the Sumatran is a browser. As it eats, it makes little squeaks through its nose and mouth.

rump. This gives it the appearance of being clothed in a tough suit of armor, a little like a medieval knight.

Like most rhinos, Javans are solitary animals. The only Javan rhinos seen together for long periods of time are females (called cows) and their young calves. Each adult male has its own territory, which it marks by spraying its urine, which is orange, on bushes. Male Javan rhinos also mark their areas by leaving their droppings in special heaps, which can be 30 feet (9 m) across.

Another way to tell where a Javan rhino has been is to look for fallen trees. Javan rhinos often flatten young trees in order to eat the tender leaves and shoots at the top. They do this by first leaning on the tree with their shoulders,

A Javan rhino feeds deep in its rainforest home. The people of Java, in Indonesia, once thought this rhino could eat fire.

using all their weight, and then pushing down on it with their front legs until the trunk bends or snaps. These forest-dwelling rhinos will also eat fruit, such as mangoes and figs, that have fallen to the ground.

Of all the rhinos, the Javan rhino is the closest to becoming extinct. There are now less than 100 of these animals in the world. Between 55 and 60 are known to live in the Ujong Kulon National Park on the island of Java. A further 10 to 15 are thought to be living along the Dong Nai River in south-central Vietnam. Sadly, this means that the Javan rhino is not only the most endangered rhino, but also the rarest large mammal in the world.

Javan rhinos used to be killed as pests. In the eighteenth century more than 500 were wiped out in two years.

The Indian rhino is very similar to the Javan rhino. It, too, has just one horn. And with its thick, gray, folded skin covered with warty bumps, it also looks as if it is wearing a suit of armor. However, the Indian rhino is bigger than the Javan species, and its horn may grow up to 24 inches (61 cm) long. The Indian rhino is the largest rhino in Asia, with males usually a little larger than females. A male can measure up to 12½ feet (3.8 m) long and weigh as much as 4850 pounds (2200 kg). Females seldom weigh more than 3500 pounds (1600 kg).

The Indian rhino is both a browser and a grazer. Like the black, Sumatran, and Javan species, it has a long upper lip

Areas where Asian rhinos can be found

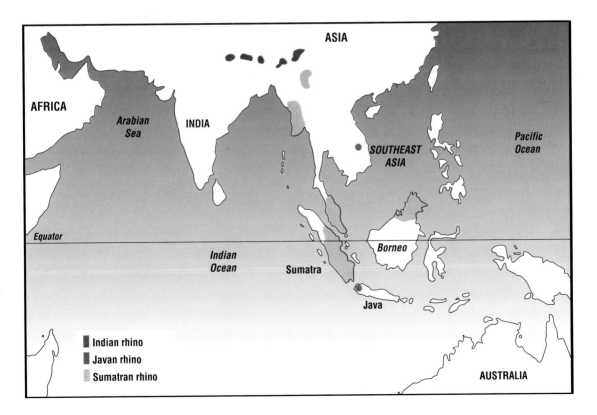

Asian Rhinos

for browsing on its favorite foods – elephant grass and other water plants and bamboo shoots. When it wants to graze on shorter grass it simply folds this lip away. Indian rhinos have often been seen plunging their heads completely underwater and tearing parts off water plants or pulling them up by their roots. And they have made themselves unpopular with many local people because they will enter farmland to eat crops, such as wheat and lentils.

   Indian rhinos are particularly fond of water. They spend most of their day in wet grasslands and swampy areas by the edges of rivers, where they wallow among the thick reed and elephant-grass beds. Indian rhinos are partly

An Indian rhino chews a mouthful of elephant grass. Indian rhinos usually feed early in the morning and at night.

sociable and partly solitary. They are willing to share waterholes and wallows with others of their kind. But if an Indian rhino enters another's feeding or sleeping area, it will be challenged by the owner, and a fight may start. Unlike African rhinos, which use their front horns as weapons, Asian rhinos fight with their teeth. Like horns, these can cause serious injuries.

Indian rhinos once had a wide range in Asia, stretching from Pakistan east to Myanmar, where they lived close to the Indus, Ganges, and Brahmaputra rivers. Today there are fewer than 2000 Indian rhinos left, found only in ten protected parks in India and Nepal.

This Indian rhino is feeding as it wallows. Despite their thick skin, Indian rhinos can become sunburnt, so they spend the hottest parts of the day in the water.

Saving Rhinos

People have been solely responsible for the fall in the number of rhinos. The Sumatran and Javan rhinos have lost much of their rainforest home, because people have cut down trees to use the timber for building and the land for farming. Indian rhinos and their human neighbors have long been in conflict – the rhinos often ate crops, so people shot the rhinos as pests. By the early twentieth century, the Indian rhino survived only in protected areas. In Africa,

The skeleton of a black rhino killed for its horns lies in Tsavo National Park in Kenya.

meanwhile, rhinos were killed by trophy hunters during the late nineteenth and early twentieth centuries.

However, by far the worst threat to rhinos has come from human beings hunting them for their horns, which are used to make medicines and dagger handles. In order to take the horn from a rhino, the hunters kill the animal first.

For hundreds of years, powdered rhino horn has been an important ingredient in traditional eastern medicines, used to treat colds, headaches, fevers, and skin diseases. And, although there is no proof that the horn can heal, people will still pay a high price for it. In 1990, about 2 pounds (1 kg) of rhino horn could be sold for $54,000 in Taiwan, South Korea, Thailand, or China.

A wildlife worker helps to capture a white rhino in South Africa. The rhino, which has been drugged to make it sleepy, will be moved to a part of Africa from which the species has disappeared.

In the Middle Eastern country of Yemen, rhino horn is carved and made into expensive, ornamental handles for special daggers worn by young Yemeni men. Between 1969 and 1977, the horns of almost 8000 rhinos were imported into North Yemen alone.

All species of rhinos are at risk, but the news is not all bad. In recent years, organizations such as the World Wildlife Fund (WWF) and the Environmental Investigation Agency (EIA) have set up campaigns to save rhinos. Many of these aim to gather information about the buying and selling of rhino horn and to persuade governments and ordinary people that what is happening should be stopped. The campaigners have had some success. The governments

A group of white rhinos from South Africa graze in their new home – Kenya's Lake Nakuru National Park.

of Yemen, Singapore, and Taiwan have banned trade in rhino horn within their countries. However, **poaching** and smuggling are still big problems.

Conservationists have tried several ways to stop people from poaching. One of these is to move rhinos from places where they are in danger to a protected area, where they are a little safer. Unfortunately, this is not a perfect solution, since moving a rhino can sometimes upset the animal so much that it dies.

The authorities have also tried to stop poaching by shooting people on sight if they are caught taking rhino

When their mothers are killed by poachers, young rhinos are helpless. Some lucky calves are found and taken to sanctuaries where they are looked after. Here two keepers give a black rhino a dust bath.

horns. One such campaign, "Operation Stronghold," has been in effect in Zimbabwe since 1984, but it does not seem to have frightened the poachers enough to stop them from killing rhinos.

Yet another method of saving rhinos from illegal hunters is to remove the animals' horns, so that poachers have no reason to kill the rhinos once they have tracked them down. This type of program was first set up in the southern African country of Namibia in 1989. Called "Operation

Two Namibian wildlife officers "dehorn" a black rhino to make it worthless to poachers. They first drug the rhino and then saw off the horns before it wakes up.

Bicornis," it was extremely successful. The only drawback to this method is that the horns eventually grow back, so the rhinos have to be "dehorned" regularly.

As a result of all these programs, rhino numbers in a few small populations have been slowly rising. For example, in Namibia, the number of black rhinos increased from 300 in 1980 to 500 in 1992. And between the 1960s and the early 1990s, the number of Indian rhinos in Nepal rose from about 80 to more than 400. This is great news, but with the world total of rhinos still less than 11,000, more needs to be done before these awesome giants will be safe.

A white rhino and her calf. White rhinos can live to be 45 years old if they are given the chance. Indian rhinos may live to be 50.

Useful Addresses

For more information about rhinoceroses and how you can help protect them, contact these organizations:

African Wildlife Foundation
1717 Massachusetts Avenue NW
Suite 602
Washington, D.C. 20036

Kenya Wildlife Fund
P.O. Box 2445, Station B
Richmond Hill
Ontario L4E 1A5

National Wildlife Federation
Attn: Ranger Rick Correspondence
Division
8925 Leesburg Pike
Vienna, Virginia 22184

U.S. Fish and Wildlife Service
Endangered Species and Habitat
Conservation
400 Arlington Square
18th and C Streets NW
Washington, D.C. 20240

Wildlife Preservation Trust International
3400 W. Girard Avenue
Philadelphia, Pennsylvania 19104

World Wildlife Fund
1250 24th Street NW
Washington, D.C. 20037

Further Reading

A Rhino Comes to America Thane Maynard (New York: Franklin Watts, 1993)

Animals in Danger Marcus Schneck (New York: Gallery Books, 1990)

Endangered Wildlife of the World (New York: Marshall Cavendish Corporation, 1993)

Extremely Weird Endangered Animals Sarah Lovett (Santa Fe, New Mexico: John Muir Publications, 1992)

Mission Rhino Jen. Bailey (Austin, Texas: Raintree-Steck Vaughn, 1994)

Rhinos: Endangered Species Malcolm Penny (New York: Facts On File, 1988)

Saving Endangered Mammals: A Field Guide to Some of the Earth's Rarest Animals Thane Maynard (New York: Franklin Watts, 1992)

Wildlife of the World (New York: Marshall Cavendish Corporation, 1994)

Glossary

Adapt: To change in order to survive in new conditions.

Browse: To feed on the leaves, shoots, and twigs of plants, bushes, and trees.

Conservationist (Kon-ser-VAY-shun-ist): A person who protects and preserves the Earth's natural resources, such as animals, plants, and soil.

Extinct (Ex-TINKT): No longer living anywhere in the world.

Graze: To feed on grass.

Habitat: The place where an animal lives. For example, the Javan rhino's habitat is the rainforest.

Herbivore (HER-biv-or): A kind of animal that eats plants rather than animals.

Mammal: A kind of animal that is warm-blooded and has a backbone. Most are covered with fur or have hair. Females have glands that produce milk to feed their young.

Mate: When a male and female get together to produce young.

Poaching: Illegal hunting.

Rainforest: A forest that has heavy rainfall much of the year.

Range: The area in the world in which a particular species of animal can be found.

Reptile: A kind of cold-blooded animal that has a backbone and is covered with scales. Lizards, snakes, and crocodiles are reptiles.

Species: A kind of animal or plant. For example, the white rhino is a species of rhino.

Subspecies: A group within a species. For example, the southern white rhino is a subspecies of the white rhino.

Territory: The piece of land in which an animal lives. Some rhinos live in territories, which they defend against others of their own kind.

Tropical: Having to do with or found in the tropics, the warm region of the Earth near the Equator.

Index